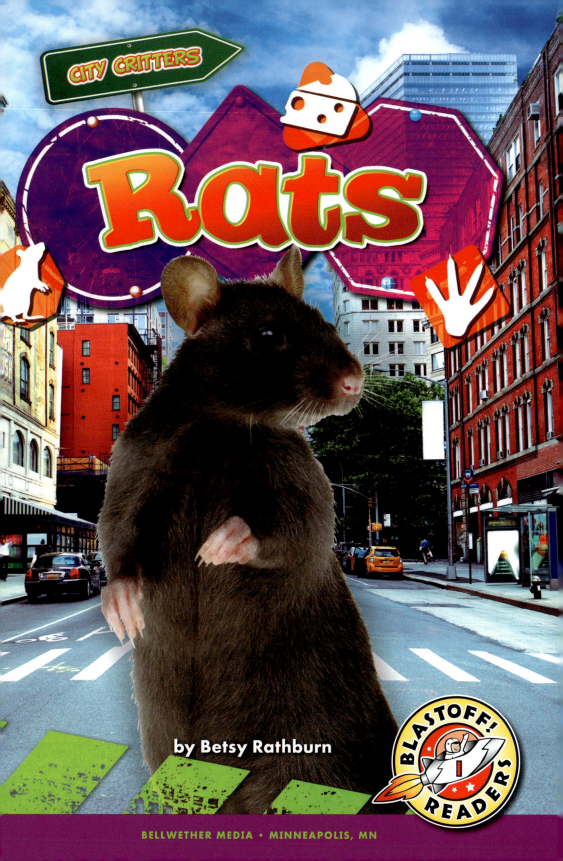

Blastoff! Readers are carefully developed by literacy experts to build reading stamina and move students toward fluency by combining standards-based content with developmentally appropriate text.

Level 1 provides the most support through repetition of high-frequency words, light text, predictable sentence patterns, and strong visual support.

Level 2 offers early readers a bit more challenge through varied sentences, increased text load, and text-supportive special features.

Level 3 advances early-fluent readers toward fluency through increased text load, less reliance on photos, advancing concepts, longer sentences, and more complex special features.

★ **Blastoff! Universe**

This edition first published in 2025 by Bellwether Media, Inc.

No part of this publication may be reproduced in whole or in part without written permission of the publisher. For information regarding permission, write to Bellwether Media, Inc., Attention: Permissions Department, 6012 Blue Circle Drive, Minnetonka, MN 55343.

Library of Congress Cataloging-in-Publication Data

LC record for Rats available at: https://lccn.loc.gov/2024035392

Text copyright © 2025 by Bellwether Media, Inc. BLASTOFF! READERS and associated logos are trademarks and/or registered trademarks of Bellwether Media, Inc.

Editor: Christina Leaf   Designer: Gabriel Hilger

Printed in the United States of America, North Mankato, MN.

Table of Contents

What Are Rats?	4
Rats in the City	10
Rats and People	18
Glossary	22
To Learn More	23
Index	24

What Are Rats?

Rats are furry **rodents**. They live near people. They are common in cities.

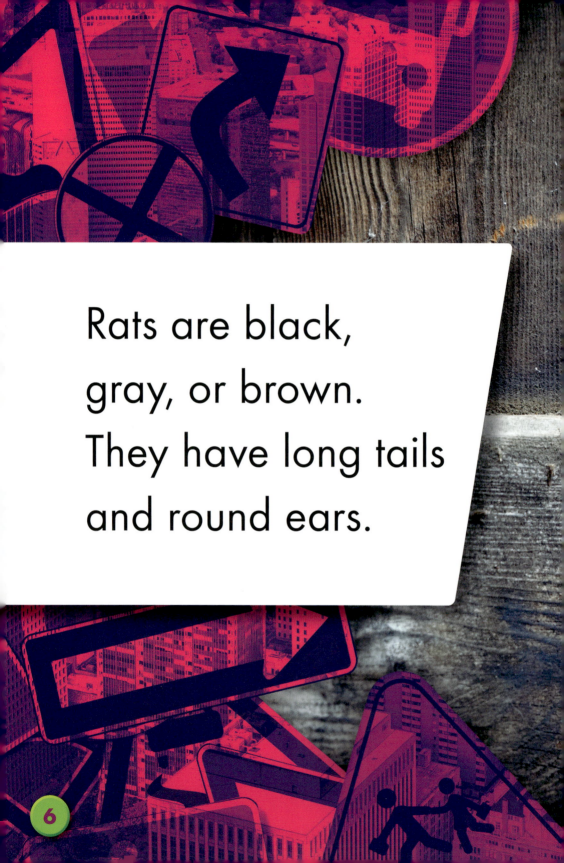

Rats are black, gray, or brown. They have long tails and round ears.

Pointed noses help them smell well. **Whiskers** help them **sense** danger.

Rats in the City

Rats live in groups called **colonies**. They make nests in dark places.

They live in many places. They often live in **attics**, basements, and **sewers**.

Rat Homes

attics | basements | sewers

Rats look for meat and fruit. They eat people food, too.

They watch for birds and cats. They bite if danger gets too close!

Rats and People

Rats make nests in people's homes. They may cause problems.

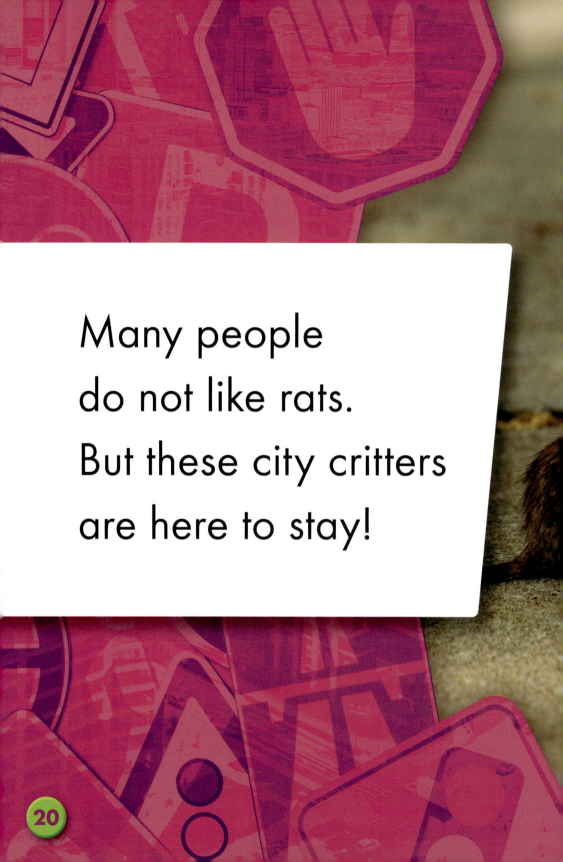

Many people do not like rats. But these city critters are here to stay!

Glossary

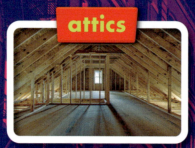

attics: spaces below the roofs of buildings

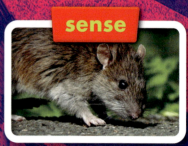

sense: to learn something through touch, smell, taste, sight, or hearing

colonies: groups of rats

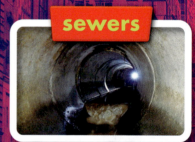

sewers: underground places that carry away wastewater

rodents: small animals that gnaw on their food

whiskers: long, stiff hairs that grow near the mouths of some animals

To Learn More

AT THE LIBRARY

Betances, Roberto. *Rats Eat Toenails!* New York, N.Y.: Gareth Stevens Publishing, 2018.

Lim, Angela. *Rat Behavior*. Minneapolis, Minn.: Abdo Publishing, 2024.

Podmorow, Ava. *Rats: Animals in the City*. Oliver, B.C.: Engage Books, 2022.

ON THE WEB

FACTSURFER

Factsurfer.com gives you a safe, fun way to find more information.

1. Go to www.factsurfer.com.

2. Enter "rats" into the search box and click 🔍.

3. Select your book cover to see a list of related content.

Index

attics, 12
basements, 12
birds, 16
bite, 16
cats, 16
cities, 4, 20
colonies, 10, 11
colors, 6
common city
  rats, 7
danger, 8, 16
ears, 6, 7
food, 14, 15
homes, 13, 18

nests, 10, 11, 18
noses, 8
people, 4, 14,
  18, 20
rodents, 4
sewers, 12
smell, 8
tails, 6, 7
whiskers, 8, 9

The images in this book are reproduced through the courtesy of: irin-k, front cover (rat); Nick Starichenko, front cover (city); torook, pp. 3, 14-15; kulbabka, pp. 4-5; Holger Kirk, pp. 6-7, 8-9; Eric Isselee, p. 7 (brown rat, black rat); aluxum, pp. 10-11; mauritius images GmbH/ Alamy Stock Photo, p. 11 (nest); Erni, pp. 12-13; Delpixart, p. 13 (attics); ronstik, p. 13 (basements); Vladimir Mulder, pp. 13 (sewers), 22 (sewers); lnzyx, p. 15 (meat); Pascal Huot, p. 15 (fruit); Erhan Inga, p. 15 (people food); Victorburnside, pp. 16-17; Nils Jacobi, p. 17 (cat); A & J Visage/ Alamy Stock Photo, pp. 18-19; imageBROKER.com GmbH & Co. KG/ Alamy Stock Photo, pp. 20-21; BryanChavezPhotography, p. 22 (attics); Nigel Harris, p. 22 (colonies); Ihor Hvozdetskyi, p. 22 (rodents); Nigel J. Harris, p. 22 (sense); Kristine Rad, p. 22 (whiskers).